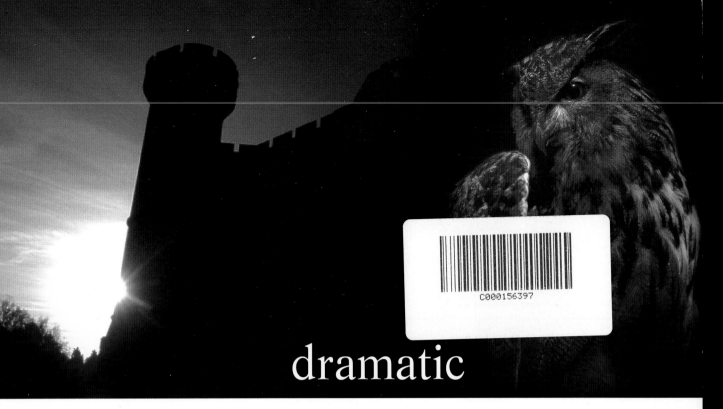

dramatic

fairytale

castle

C·O·N·T·E·N·T·S

INTRODUCTION to Eastnor Castle
by James Hervey-Bathurst   4
CONSTRUCTION and Decoration of the Castle   6
RESTORATION of the Castle Interiors: 10
My Approach by Sarah Hervey-Bathurst
THE FAMILY STORY by James Hervey-Bathurst   14

THE TOUR
Entrance Hall   17
Great Hall   18
Red or Inner Hall   22
Dining Room   24
Gothic Drawing Room   26
Octagon Saloon   28
Long Library   30
Turret Room   32
Little Library   32
Staircase Hall   34
Chinese Bedroom   36
Chapel   37
Guest Bedroom Landing   38
Red Bedroom   38
Red Dressing Room   40
Landing and Bathroom   40
Italian Bedroom   41
Blue Double Bedroom   41
State Bedroom (downstairs)   42
Arboretum and Deer Park   44

EASTNOR CASTLE - an architectural summary   46

FAMILY LINE OF DESCENT   48

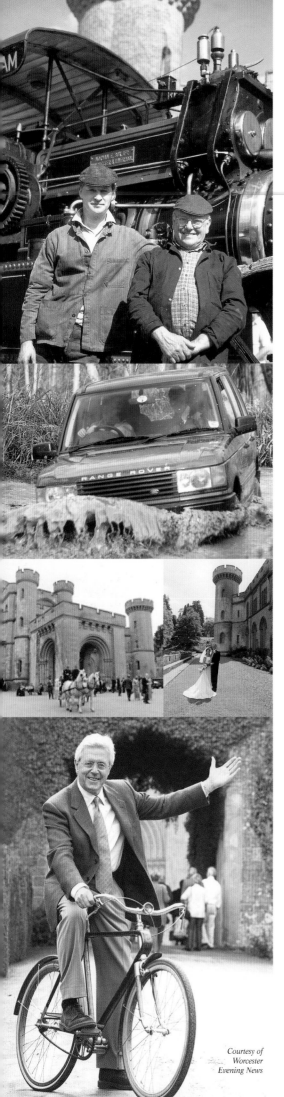

INTRODUCTION

We are very fortunate that this Castle still remains our family home and we are delighted to welcome all our visitors.

Much has changed in the last ten years. When I was brought up here, in the smaller rooms which still constitute our family apartments, I never thought it would be possible to bring the state rooms back to life and recolonise the seven bedrooms with their bathrooms that were abandoned in 1939. But I underestimated the vision and determination of my wife, Sarah, who saw the potential of restoring the house to its former splendour, even though much of the decoration and furniture was rundown or damaged. The results fully justify her decision to undertake this massive task.

During much of the last 10 years, I have been away working in Birmingham and London, but gradually Sarah and the many craftsmen, builders and decorators we have used have brought this exciting project to completion. When we remember to book in time, we can invite our friends and their children to stay and all enjoy the space and the atmosphere. It means a great deal to us to be able to do this, and visitors appreciate the house all the more for it.

Otherwise, Eastnor is used for conferences, weddings, wedding receptions, dinners, concerts etc. We have had films such as Little Lord Fauntleroy made here, and we have regularly been used by Land Rover over the last 25 years to entertain their guests on the way to or from demanding off-road driving in our woods and hills.

It has been great fun – and very hard work – making the house alive again. It is also very rewarding to see our guests and visitors enjoying themselves in the ways that were intended when Eastnor was originally built.

Top: Premier steeplejack and television personality Fred Dibnah at an Eastnor Castle's annual Steam Fair and Country Show.

Below: A Land Rover off-road driving day on the Eastnor Castle Estate.

Above left: Eastnor Castle makes a spectacular venue for civil weddings and receptions.

Left: Presenter Michael Aspel at Eastnor Castle, for BBC Television's 'Antiques Roadshow', July 2000.

Courtesy of Worcester Evening News

CONSTRUCTION
and Decoration of the Castle

Eastnor Castle was built by the 2nd Baron Somers, later 1st Earl, between 1810 and 1824. The combination of inherited wealth and a judicious marriage to the daughter of the eminent and rich Worcestershire historian, Dr Treadway Nash, enabled the 1st Earl to commission the building of a family home to impress his contemporaries and pitch his family into the higher ranks of the ruling class for future generations. Then, as now, the size and splendour of a country house were obvious indicators of the standing and fortune of any family.

The style proposed by his architect, the young Robert Smirke, was Norman Revival. From a distance, Eastnor tried to create the impression of an Edward 1st-style medieval fortress guarding the Welsh Borders. It was an assertion of power in a period of fear and uncertainty following the French Revolution and the Napoleonic wars.

Watercolour of Eastnor Castle as proposed by the architect.

The symmetry of the design emphasized authority, distinguishing it from the more rambling, picturesque, castellated mansions of a slightly earlier period at Downton Castle (Shropshire) and Smirke's 1805 creation for the Earl of Lonsdale at Lowther Castle (Cumbria).

By any standards, the castle is massive, and the construction team and materials used were on a similar scale. 250 men working day and night were employed over the first six years of building, and in the first 18 months 4,000 tons of building stone, 16,000 tons of mortar and 600 tons of wood were used. Stone came from sandstone quarries in the Forest of Dean by canal to Ledbury and thence by mule. Estate timber was used as much as possible, but the major roof trusses and beams were cast iron, then a relatively new material for building.

The castle cost £85,923.13s. 11d., approximately £8.5 million today. Later plans to build an orangery to conceal the servants' quarters were dropped because of a shortage of funds.

Those interiors by Smirke which the 1st Earl could afford to complete were simple and in keeping with the medieval style of the building. Architectural details remain in the Red Hall, Dining Room and Staircase Hall, but the original Gothic arches, shown in the watercolour of the Dining Room, were concealed in the 1930s when the style had became very unfashionable. The plain Gothic benches and chairs in the entrance and Great Hall were designed by Smirke, as were the turned, ebonised chairs in the Dining Room, the style of which was evocative of earlier English furniture, rather than the French influence made unfashionable by the Napoleonic Wars.

In 1849, the 2nd Earl commissioned A W N Pugin to decorate his Drawing Room in the High Gothic Revival style. A celebration of the ancient lineage of the family over the chimney-piece and thus its claim to power also evoked the medieval culture of religious feudalism from which Pugin derived his inspiration.

THE GREAT HALL - 1910

THE GOTHIC DRAWING ROOM - 1910

THE DINING ROOM - AS DESIGNED

Charles, 3rd Earl Somers, undertook more lavish
embellishments of the castle in the 1860s and 1870s,
and it is possible to trace the evolution of the taste of this
unusually artistic and educated man in various rooms,
notably the Long Library and the State Bedroom.
As the Gothic Drawing Room represented the latest style in
its time, it indicates that Charles, who was instrumental in
his father's decision to commission Pugin, was at the
forefront of contemporary taste.

THE GREAT HALL TODAY

The Octagon Room, in contrast, was classical in design
and originally decorated in cream and crimson silk, hung
with classical prints and filled with Louis XVI furniture.
It exhibited the top end of conventional English good taste.
The Chinese Bedroom, although quite different in style,
also reflects the status and obvious good taste of the owner.

Developing out of an interest in classical antiquities
collected in Mesopotamia and an enduring love of the
Mediterranean, Charles started buying 17th century Italian
furniture, Flemish tapestries, medieval armour and 15th-
century art of the Renaissance. This catholic approach to
collecting was considered avant garde at a time when
contemporary furniture was still considered the most
desirable. The 3rd Earl created appropriately Italianate
settings for his collection, in particular, in the Little
Library, where the 17th century bookcases were bought
from the Academy of the Intronati in Siena. He bought
almost no Victorian furniture and no Victorian art with the
exception of work by the painter, G F Watts. Both men
shared a love of Venetian art and its use of lambent colour,
which inspired both Watts' painting and the 3rd Earl's
decoration.

THE GOTHIC DRAWING ROOM TODAY

Over time, much of this rich colour had faded. It has been
our aim to restore this to the Castle in keeping with the
original spirit of the place.

THE DINING ROOM TODAY

The Restoration of the Castle Interiors: My Approach

by Sarah Hervey-Bathurst

In September 1939, the traditional aristocratic way of life at Eastnor Castle came to an end and the Castle was offered to the Australian High Commission in case it needed to leave London after the Blitz. The contents were put into store. The family retreated, first to a cottage in the grounds and, after the war, restricted themselves to the smaller, private rooms of the castle where they lived carefully and quietly, putting their energies into farming and modernising the other estate properties, which seemed to offer the more promising future.

The Castle came, quite rightly, low on the list of priorities. Repairs, if they were undertaken at all, had to be carried out with a short-term, make-do approach, which inevitably meant that survival in the castle became almost a full-time struggle.

In winter, collecting wood for wood-burning stoves, stoking the straw-burning boiler, unfreezing pipes, clearing the roofs of snow and leaves, which otherwise blocked the internal drains and led to flooding, and in summer, patrolling with buckets when it rained to catch the water seeping through the old lead or its crumbling asphalt replacement or simply the 50 yard hike from the bedrooms to the single bathroom to find the basin inevitably shared by the washing machine drain pipe were all features of those days. Despite that relative discomfort, lack of funds and the pressure of hard work, James's family had a great attachment to and pride in the place. Like any home of this scale, they tended to define themselves by it and were (in turn) shaped by it.

BEFORE and AFTER:
One of the Castle's bedrooms in 1986 before restoration, and opposite, how it appears today, as accommodation for private and corporate guests.

When my mother-in-law, to whom the castle and estate belonged, died in 1986, it was natural that James, as her elder son, should want to live here, but also natural that he and I should seek to take advantage of the greater public interest in historic houses and commercial opportunities they offered by gradually restoring the principal interiors and making Eastnor a viable place in which both to live and work.

Most houses, of course, develop out of basic needs, but Eastnor combines basic needs with pure fantasy; the child in everyone dreams of a castle like this, and suddenly here it is. The sheer force of its personality that made the dream come true is so strong that it nearly knocked me over when I first started.

Castles, of course, are aggressive, which is what gives them their energy, but they are also protective, the safest and most secure places you can imagine, and it is this protective aspect of strength which makes castles so compelling –

know it intimately and discover what it was all about.

I had read English at university and I loved the way the castle was packed with original source material: letters, books, clothes, furniture and paintings, all of which had been created, chosen personally or used by someone to say something about themselves. These things could now reflect back their personality, attitude, loves and aspirations and, by responding to this, I could return to these works of art the meaning they had lost. Practically speaking,

and romantic. They seem to contain the resolution of those opposites normally considered irreconcilable: strength and weakness, male and female, life and death, love and war, but the balance is a very delicate one.

When we moved in, much of the castle had not been inhabited for 50 years; as a result the human connection had been broken, the balance lost, and it was a negative and hostile place. I wanted to feel at home and to relate to the place and I felt sure that, if I did, others would too. This was the impetus behind the restoration, but the first thing was to get to

this meant that a picture badly hung in an ill-considered situation, out of context, was like putting a tender plant in freezing temperatures. It didn't stand a chance.

Discovering this secret life of works of art and restoring it led naturally to the arrangement of rooms. Simultaneously, I developed an understanding of architecture: the classical precepts and the way Gothic expands upon these by allowing the eye and mind to soar, and the relationship between architecture and decoration, the latter always being subordinate, making 'taste' simply what is appropriate.

These, combined with a knowledge of historical colour and textiles, were important because they provided structure and reference points. But technical expertise alone cannot breathe life into stones and space. For this you need 'heart': an honest response to your surroundings. I find it in nature where it is true to itself: here in the thorn scrub, oak wood, rocks and extraordinary lights of the Malvern Hills and also in the elemental landscape of the Yorkshire Moors where I was brought up. This characteristic requires no training. I believe everyone has the ability to recognise immediately

needs and then imagined a piece of furniture, a picture or a fabric in them. We tried lots of different pieces in lots of different places and eventually things began to fall into place, but it is also an on-going process. When we can, we add things to 'dress' the rooms, old fabrics, which sadly have a limited life, are replaced with new ones on cushions or chair covers and, most exciting, one thing which has long been away at the restorers is returned to the rightful place starting a cascade of alterations in the room as everything has to be adjusted to accommodate it.

and instinctively a room that is right (and a room that is wrong) but they don't trust the instinct enough to have the confidence to develop it. It is most lost or hidden in those noisy people who tell you how things 'ought' to be.

This was my approach to restoring Eastnor. I sought to change the atmosphere by bringing my heart and mind to every corner and aspect of each room. I eliminated everything that was bad – bad design, poor execution and anything false or phoney, done for effect or to impress or show off. I got rid of the clutter and then spent time 'absorbing' the rooms. I recognised the rooms'

'Heart' and hard work have restored Eastnor to itself and made it a home again. If our visitors feel that as they absorb its atmosphere, I shall be delighted.

THE FAMILY STORY

by James Hervey-Bathurst

My mother's ancestors, the Cocks family, moved to Eastnor at the end of the 16th century. They bought the manor of Castleditch, an engraving of which is in the Great Hall, and over the following 200 years gradually accumulated further land in this area.

The Cocks married into the Worcestershire-based Somers family, and the combination of their estates with the valuable inheritance passed down by the Lord Chancellor Somers in the early 18th century, the banking wealth of the Cocks Biddulph bank (now incorporated into Barclays), and the sale of his father's estate at Dumbleton, near Evesham, gave the 1st Earl Somers the means to start building the castle in 1812. His family, distinguished in law, politics and the army, needed a new residence more in keeping with its status.

Despite the then massive building costs of over £80,000, the family continued to prosper in the 19th century up to the time of the 1870s' agricultural depression. At that time, the Somers Cocks' estates exceeded 13,000 acres, and the family also owned Somers Town in London and Reigate Priory in Surrey (gifts to the Lord Chancellor by William III). Then, as income from rents dropped and the 1st Earl's great-granddaughter, Lady Henry Somerset, began to direct her energies and wealth towards charitable purposes, the family fortunes started to decline, as did those of many other landed aristocrats who lacked income from urban property, coal or industry.

In 1920 my grandfather, the last Lord Somers to live here (the earldom became extinct in 1883 on the death of his cousin) inherited the estate, by which time it was somewhat reduced. In 1926, he was appointed Governor of Victoria, Australia, and the castle was left empty as, not surprisingly, it had proved difficult to let. On my grandparents' return in 1930, however, having saved some of the Governor's annual £5000 tax-free allowance, they were able to install some much-needed central heating and decorate various rooms, including the bathroom next to what is now the Queen's Bedroom for the visit of Queen Mary in 1937. Generally, however, this was a difficult time during the 1930s' agricultural depression.

On the outbreak of war in 1939, most of the house was emptied as it was no longer appropriate to live there, and there was a possibility that it could be used for other purposes. We were probably fortunate that eventually no one decided to move in and the damage suffered by so many other houses was avoided.

My grandfather died in 1944, having become Chief Scout as successor to Baden-Powell in 1940. Although hard hit by death duties, my grandmother moved back in greatly altered circumstances in 1945 and my parents took over in 1949. My brother and I were brought up here and thoroughly enjoyed ourselves as boys, bicycling round the then sparsely furnished state rooms on rainy days and playing badminton in the Hall.

There is no doubt that the 1950s, 60s and 70s were not easy for the owners of stately homes, and many owners gave up, and houses were sold or abandoned. My mother used to say that she considered demolishing Eastnor but gave the idea up when told the cost. We are lucky she was careful with her money and that she also did not strip out all the contents of the rooms we were no longer using. She was successful, nevertheless, in keeping the basic fabric intact, whilst investing any surplus income from the estate in other areas. My father managed the farm and also introduced Land Rover to the estate.

When Sarah and I moved here in 1989, we were presented with a wonderful but daunting challenge. As English Heritage were able to grant-aid the necessary repairs to the exterior - we have received over £400,000 to date - we could allocate more of our resources to start to bring the interiors back to life. Now that most of the work is done, we are fortunate to have a devoted staff both to look after our guests and the house, inside and outside, and also to develop our various activities. We are proud to welcome you here and thank you for coming.

THE TOUR

Entrance Hall

This imposing entrance is flanked by portraits of
1st Earl Somers on the left (Harrison), the
builder of the house, and by the 12th Earl, later
Duke, of Shrewsbury (Kneller) on the right.
Lord Shrewsbury was a great friend of John
Somers, the Lord Chancellor, from whom the
original distinction and wealth of the family were
derived. The Somers' family had married into
the Cocks, who had owned land at Eastnor since
1600. The wooden benches and chairs, which
are early Gothic in style, were made to Smirke's
design for the house. The medieval suits of
armour are part of the collection acquired by the
family in the 1870s; those at the top of the stairs
are from Nuremberg and were possibly looted by
Napoleon from the Elector of Hanover.

The hall was redecorated in 1989 but the
unusual 19th century frieze was retained.
The umbrella stand is part of an old section of
elm drain recovered from roadworks in
Mayfair, London.

Lord Chancellor Somers

*John Cocks, 1st Earl Somers,
builder of the Castle.*

The Great Hall

An early watercolour confirms that this was intended to be the symbolic heart of the baronial castle. Using its scale to impress, this room would be opened from time to time for the entertainment of tenants and employees, when trestle tables and benches would be brought in for the purpose. As early photographs show, however, the room was gradually embellished and decorated, not by George Gilbert Scott as was once planned but by the less well known G E Fox, who introduced the marble columns in the gallery and painted wall decoration, said to be taken from the design on a Saracen banner captured in the Crusades and preserved as an altar cloth in Toulouse Cathedral.

It was intended that most of the principal decoration in the hall should be armour and weapons, very much like the hall of a genuine castle. When the room was rearranged in 1989 under the guidance of Professor Bernard Nevill, much of the armour was removed to the Red Hall and only 12 suits remain. These were part of a collection of 33 suits bought by the 3rd Earl Somers in Milan in 1853 and may have been used by the bodyguard of Emperor Charles V.

In its present state, replicating an Edwardian living hall, the Hall is used as a drawing room. The ottoman, sofas and armchairs are all new (Howard Chairs, Camden) but covered with old fabric. The portraits on the left-hand side as you enter mostly depict various members of the family but also include Elizabeth of Bohemia (Miereveldt), sister of Charles I, whose portrait hangs opposite. On the right of the right-hand fireplace is a small portrait of William of Orange by Cornelius Janssens. This was given by the King to Lord Chancellor Somers, who had proved the legal validity of the proof of succession. The

This huge space, now transformed into a grand drawing room, takes ten hours to heat up to a comfortable 20°C.

ebony cabinet on the left of the entrance hall door was also given to the Lord Chancellor by his friend, Lord Shrewsbury.

Details of two portraits in the Hall, Persian School, 17th century.

Courtesy of the Courtauld Institute of Art

William of Orange, as a child, by Cornelius Janssens.

Courtesy of the Courtauld Institute of Art

The carved chairs with gilded leather seats are part of the collection of Venetian 17th century furniture. Above the entrance door is a minstrels' gallery.

The Red or Inner Hall

The 3rd Earl was susceptible to what he called 'armouritis' and in the 1870s bought half of the famous Meyrick Collection of medieval armour from Goodrich Court near Ross on Wye, the remainder going to the Wallace Collection. Ancient tales of chivalry and romance appealed strongly to the Victorians, offering a nostalgic return to an age of fixed codes and values, in contrast to the rapidly changing world around them. The shields around the Hall door are 14th century Austrian pavises, used to shelter crossbowmen when re-arming their weapons. The Dutch clock is 18th century: the knight on horseback is Italian with the Visconti crest on his shield.

The ceiling was redecorated in 1991 when the panels were painted with crests of families related to the Somers and the Cocks in the 20th century, to carry through the heraldic theme of the two adjoining rooms. The mouldings are part of the original decoration for the house by Smirke.

 The 3rd Earl Somers amassed this important collection in the mid 19th century to complete the decoration of the room. He complained that he suffered from 'armouritis'.

The Dining Room

Smirke originally provided Gothic arches at each end and over the doors. These were removed by Lady Somers in 1933 both to conceal the detail and to create a better space for pictures. The room was redecorated in 1990 when new curtains and curtain poles were fitted and the mirrors and additional pictures brought in from other rooms or purchased.

We used 180 metres of fabric for the new curtains and chair covers. The mirror came from a former Salvation Army hostel.

The original dining-room table leaves were missing and so new ones of Spanish rather than Cuban mahogany were commissioned. The chairs, benches and fire screens were also designed by Smirke for the room. The portraits of Archbishop Tillotson, Queen Henrietta Maria and the Countess of Bedford formed part of the 17th century collection of Lord Chancellor Somers, who is also depicted. The family portraits include a full-length Romney of the 1st Earl and, at the opposite end of the room, his younger half-brother, Philip Cocks, at the age of five. Philip Cocks is the great-great-great grandfather of the present owner. Officers who fought with Wellington are represented by Sir Felton Hervey, later an ADC to Wellington, and Edward Charles Cocks, an intelligence officer and elder son of the 1st Earl, who died at the siege of Burgos. The obelisk in the park was erected in 1812 in his memory.

The ceiling was decorated in the 1850s and features crests of families with which the Somers and Cocks were either closely or tenuously linked.

The Dining Room is used regularly now, both for corporate and private functions, and has a modern kitchen adjacent, which is some 50 metres closer than the original in the service wing, which served the house until 1920 and is now the tea room.

The Gothic Drawing Room

This room survives largely unchanged from the time when it was redecorated by the Crace Brothers to the designs of A W N Pugin for the 2nd Earl in 1849.

The work caused such a stir in the neighbourhood that it was believed Queen Victoria was planning to visit. The massive chimney-piece and family tree provide the focus while the chairs, table, desk and bookcase were all designed by Pugin, with the Somers' 'S' and coronet inlaid in the table and bookcase doors. The chandelier was exhibited at the Great Exhibition in 1851 and made by Hardman of Birmingham from an original in a Nuremberg church. There is an identical version in the House of Commons, which formerly hung at Alton Towers.

The Brussels tapestries were a wedding present to Lady Caroline Yorke, wife of the 2nd Earl Somers: their portraits hang in the Dining Room. The portrait on the easel of Mrs Fitzherbert, morganatic wife of the Prince Regent, is by Raphael Smith. One of her nieces, Louisa Smythe, married a Hervey-Bathurst.

 Pugin, responsible for much of the original decoration in the Palace of Westminster, designed the new decoration for this room in 1849. It is now licensed for civil wedding ceremonies and is used most weekends for this purpose.

The Octagon Saloon

This room has been extensively redecorated on two occasions over the last sixty years. First, the Gothic fireplaces were removed by Lady Somers in the 1930s with only one substituted to give a single focus to the room. Fortunately, both were preserved in the cellars, rediscovered and reinstated by Estate staff in 1990, when the room was painted by the decorative artist, Laura Jeffreys. At the same time, the mirrors were added and the portraits by G F Watts gathered from elsewhere in the house and displayed together.

The chandelier is Dutch and the new carpet, replacing a similar one to those in the Long Library and Little Library woven in India, was machine-made for the room in China in 1994. The portraits include Ellen Terry, the actress who was briefly married to Watts, 3rd Earl Somers, a friend of the artist (portrait above the Library door) and his daughters, Lady Henry Somerset and her sister.

A portrait of the 3rd Earl Somer's wife, Virginia Pattle, hangs opposite, and, to the left of the Library entrance, Tennyson, the Poet Laureate, godfather of Arthur, 6th Lord Somers.

 We found the two fireplaces stored in the cellar where they had been put in 1932, when the room was redecorated and one, larger fireplace installed. My grandmother's idea was to keep the ladies and gentlemen together in the same part of the room after dinner.

The Long Library

Designed by the decorator G E Fox, to the 3rd Earl's specification, the shelving and inlaid woodwork were made in Italy and assembled on site by Estate workmen. The 17th century Flemish tapestries depict Catherine di Medici in a mythological allegory and came from a palazzo in Mantua. The tapestries between the windows depict mythical scenes, and the ceiling is painted with emblems of various qualities representing virtues and their corresponding vices. The chimney-pieces are of Istrian stone and also carved in Italy: the figure of Garibaldi is represented in one of the boats. The model ship was made by French prisoners in Stapleton Jail, Bristol, in 1794. It is made of bone, locks of hair and brass buttons.

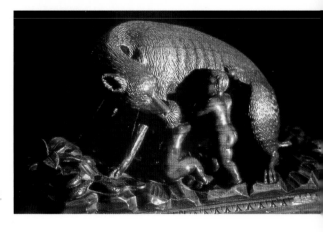

The room features several examples of fine woodcarving. On a side table, surmounting an inlaid casket, is a representation of the city of Rome's legendary founders, the two brothers, Romulus and Remus, suckling on a she-wolf. According to tradition, Romulus was the first King and founder of Rome in 753 BC.

The Cassapanca (bench) bears the Medici crest and the 17th century torchères are also Italian. There are approximately 5,000 books in the Library, many of which came from the collection of Rev. Treadway Nash, an antiquarian whose daughter was married to John, 1st Earl Somers.

Turret Room

The little room off the east corner of the Library was used by the Long Library's designer, Fox and known as 'the fox's den': it shows clearly the trefoil shape of the tower. There is a good view of the obelisk commissioned from Smirke by 1st Earl Somers on the skyline. The contents include photographs by Julia Margaret Cameron, a sister of Virginia, 3rd Countess Somers, and an Assyrian bas-relief from Nineveh, given to 3rd Earl Somers by its excavator, Henry Layard.

Photograph of Mrs Leslie Stephen, mother of the novelist Virginia Woolf and Vanessa Bell, taken by Julia Margaret Cameron, sister of the 3rd Countess and aunt of Mrs Stephen, and below, one of her photograph albums.

The Little Library

The walnut shelves came from Siena where they were bought from the assembly hall of the Academy of the Intronati. A notice on display records that they were designed by Josef Posi and date from 1624. The mirror over the chimney-piece is framed by pearwood carvings formerly at the family home in Reigate. The billiard table dates from the early 20th century and is by Burroughes and Watts. It weighs over 1 ton and was reassembled in 1990, having been put away in 1939.

This room was redecorated in 1990, using a fabric of Victorian design from Watts of Westminster, reprinted for the purpose.

*Courtesy of the
Courtauld Institute of Art*

The portrait by Watts on the far wall is of Virginia, 3rd Countess Somers, before her marriage. The 3rd Earl is said to have fallen in love with her on the strength of this painting, which he saw in Watts' studio. Half-French, Virginia came from a family of eight Pattle sisters renowned for their looks and effusive vivacity and known collectively as 'Pattledom'. One, Sarah Prinsep, held a literary salon at Little Holland House, and their niece, Mrs Leslie Stephen, was the mother of Virginia Woolf and Vanessa Bell.

Opposite Virginia, on the wall adjacent to the Long Library, is a portrait by Wootton of Queen Anne's horse, Denmark, with its groom.

The Staircase Hall

The 16th century tapestries were bought and hung here in 1990. The largest of these depicts the meeting of Antony and Cleopatra. The set of three Bruges tapestries show *Judith with the head of Holophernes, Solomon and the Queen of Sheba* and *Susannah and the Elders.*

The staircase was designed by Smirke with cast iron banisters. The bust is of Charles, 3rd Earl Somers, by Boehm. The wooden chandelier came from the Palazzo Corsini in Florence, and the hall chairs are Venetian, bearing the arms of a 17th century doge. The dragon benches are of the same period.

The mid 18th century Dutch clock by Johannes du Chesne shows Andromeda about to be rescued by Perseus.

The bird in the display case is a capercaillie, the largest game bird in the British Isles. They are still to be found in the Scottish pine forests.

Queen's Bedroom

This room and its neighbour (originally the dressing room), reflect
the enduring British fascination with the Orient. Hung with
18th century hand-painted Chinese wallpaper and furnished with
19th century furniture in the Chinese style, these were the best guest
bedrooms in the Castle and were used by Queen Mary on her
visit to Eastnor in 1937. The embroidery on the cushions was
taken from Imperial robes. Note the pigtail of human hair on
the Mandarin's hat.

The Chapel

The stained-glass windows were given to 3rd Earl
Somers and his wife by their daughters when the chapel
was converted from a bedroom in the 1880s. It was
never consecrated and was used for house prayers.
The religious pictures are from the 3rd Earl's collection
of early Italian art. The painting over the altar is by
Biagio di Antonio, a contemporary of Botticelli, and the
Madonna and child on the easel by an unknown
14th century artist.

Guest Bedroom Landing

The portraits of the 6th Lord and Lady Somers, the grandparents of the present owner, are by De Laszlo (either side of the arch). At the entrance to the landing is another portrait of Lord Somers (Birley) showing him as Chief Scout, a post he held from 1940 - 1944.

Red Bedroom

Now the best guest bedroom, it was redecorated in 1991 in homage to Lord Chancellor Somers, whose portrait hangs between the windows. The portraits of Restoration ladies displaying their charms together with the Hondecoeter painting of a cockerel crowing over his hens evoke the spirit of that age.
The furniture, with the curvaceous carving of the same period, is Venetian and French and was collected by the 3rd Earl in the 1860s.

 The fleur-de-lys wallpaper is an original Coles hand block, and the curtains were woven to match.

Lord Somers' Dressing Room

The paintings are mainly by modern and contemporary British artists, collected by James and Sarah Hervey-Bathurst. The portrait over the door is by Augustus John, that over the bed by Spencer Watson, and the paintings to the right of the bed are by Susannah Fiennes, Emma Sargeant and Howard Morgan.

Landing and Bathroom

The landscape is of the Lake of Averno by Hackaert. The portrait beyond is of Elizabeth Hervey-Bathurst, only child of 6th Lord Somers, and opposite is a portrait of her husband, Ben Hervey-Bathurst, as a child. The portrait on the right of the doorway leading to the bathroom is of James Hervey-Bathurst, their elder son. The bathroom has been recently refurbished around the original mahogany-framed lavatory with its decorated bowl by George Jennings of London, who was the contractor for all the major plumbing works at the Castle. In common with most of the restoration work in the house, the mahogany panelling was fitted by Estate staff.

Italian Bedroom

The watercolours were all painted by Charles, 3rd Earl Somers and include views of Palermo, Madeira and the Monastery of Meteora.

The wardrobe is late 19th century but the chest of drawers is Louis XIV. The dish on the chimney-piece is 17th century Maiolica.

Blue Double Bedroom

This was originally the dressing room for the Italian Room but was converted into a double room to accommodate American guests for a millennium house party.

The watercolours are also by Charles 3rd Earl Somers and include views of Algeria, Lake Como and Mount Athos, which he visited in 1843.

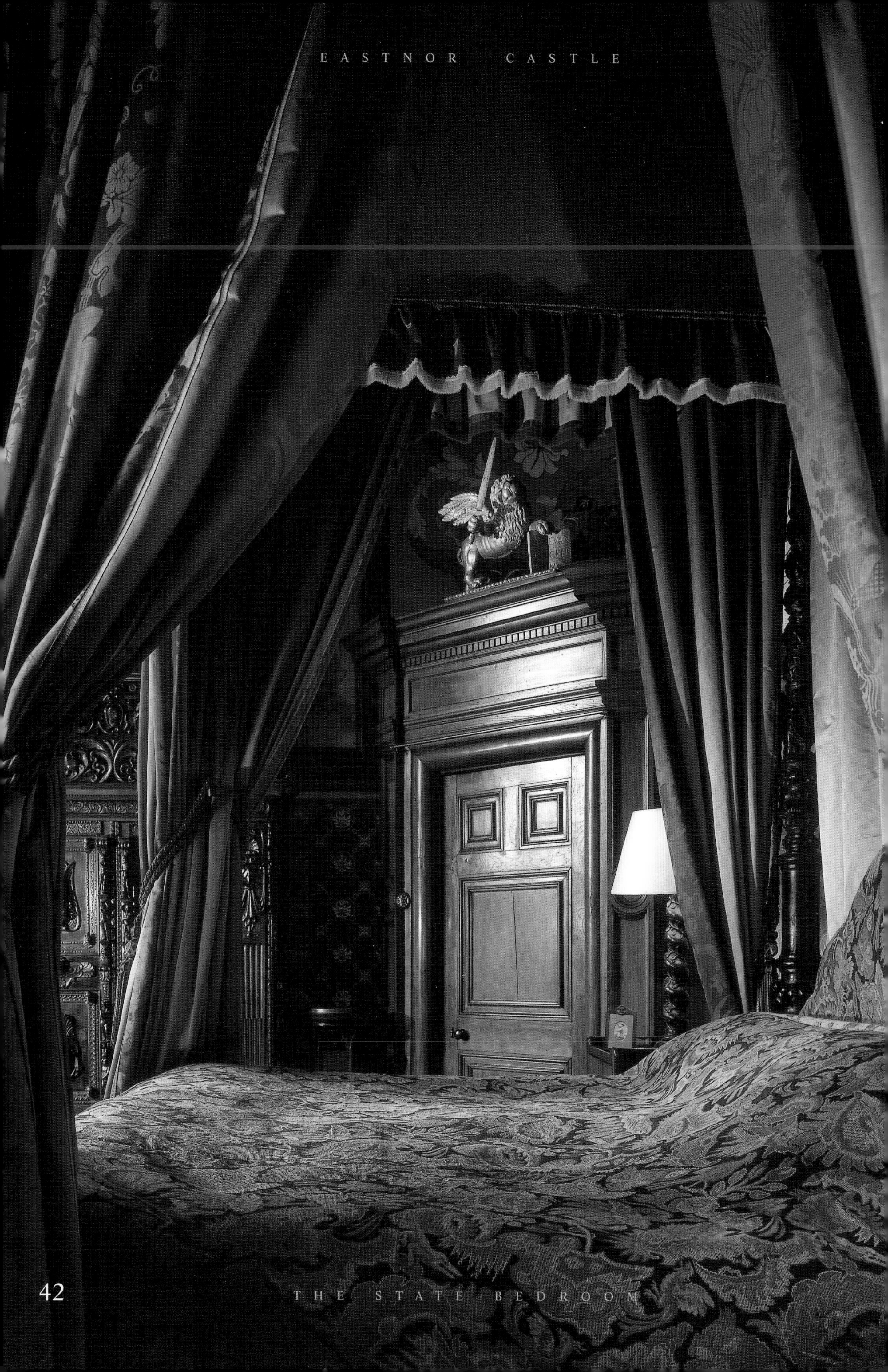

THE STATE BEDROOM

The State Bedroom

(downstairs)

This was the 3rd Earl's bedroom and is hung with panels from the Royal School of Needlework. The large altarpiece with tabernacle over the wardrobe is by Ridolfo di Ghirlandaio. *The Last Supper* is from the studio of Jacopo Bassano and *The Baptism of Christ* over the entrance by a follower of Tintoretto. The bed is Italian and belonged to Cardinal Bellarmine (17th century). The wardrobe and chest of drawers are 17th century Genoese.

 The Latin motto on the chimney piece means: 'Hope knows no defeat' - the Earl had three daughters...

The Dressing Room has been converted into a bathroom.

Arboretum and Deer Park

Castellated terraces descend to a lake created at the same time as the Castle and stocked with carp.

The remains of the family's original house, Castleditch, form one of the islands.

The Deer Park, part of a medieval chase, originally surrounded the Castle. In the 1860s and '70s the 3rd Earl created the arboretum, bringing back seed from all over the world.

Of particular interest are the magnificent, stately cedars, now at their best.

(The 3rd Earl was responsible for introducing the rangy Atlas Cedar to the British Isles). Areas of the surrounding hills were also planted with rare trees and exotic shrubs by the 3rd Earl, to enhance the romantic setting.

The buzzard is Britain's most
numerous large bird of prey, with
a wingspan of around five feet.
This beautiful bird is found
in good numbers around
Eastnor and can regularly
be seen in the Deer Park
and around the Castle
and Arboretum at any
time of the year.

EASTNOR CASTLE -
An Architectural Summary

The imposing mass and scale of Eastnor reflects, as Alistar Rowan (*Country Life*, 1968) suggests, the personality of its creator the second Baron and first Earl Somers. His portrait by Harrison shows a character self-consciously swathed in his robes with an uncritical capacity for self-dramatization. Eastnor can at first sight appear to be too big overall, and in particular too wide in relation to its height. Its plan covers an area 320 by 180ft. A desire to impress is exemplified in the 60ft high entrance hall which echoes a slightly earlier scheme at Fonthill.

Among the strangest features are the cloverleaf towers, which jut out from each of the four corners of the main building; they help to make the building seem so large, but could they have been intended to have any practical purpose?

The plan echoes the form of an 18th-century Georgian block with wings, complete with castellated detailing. Its considerable weight dominates the landscape, a reference to the controlling power of the castle in the Middle Ages and yet the house manages in its massing and outline to combine the idea of a symmetrical castle with the calculated irregularity of the picturesque. Thus, while the massing may only be a partial success, the tall east side set on its Terrace with mysteriously low tunnels passing under the corner towers to the South and North fronts, provides a dramatic experience anticipated by the works of Anne Radcliffe, author of best selling 'gothic' novels in this period.

Robert Smirke was 30 when he began the building in 1811. He was regarded as a safe and reliable pair of hands, who would complete the job on time and to budget. The papers preserved at Eastnor demonstrate this capacity for business, in revealing his control of every aspect of the building. The assured nature of the detail reflects this confidence. His use of iron roof trusses before 1820 suggests that he was quick to perceive the potential of iron. However, after a rapid start suggested by payments of £16,000 in 1812, and £25,000 in 1813, the rate of work appears to have declined in the next year to only £8,000. The large increase in 1813 was intended to speed up the work so that the family could move into the west end of the castle, though many parts must have remained little more than a shell, with only £2,000 being spent in 1817. Smirke's final bill of £82,000 is impressively close to his estimate.

Gradually in the course of the century, the large spaces were made more habitable. The Entrance Hall, Great Staircase, and Dining Room retain the original decorative scheme. The Great Hall was redecorated in a Moorish Gothic manner to house a collection of armour and the 1st Earl's Gothic Library was remodelled by Fox in the Renaissance style. Pugin began the decoration of the Gothic Drawing Room after the work at the House of Lords was completed in 1847. He was much in demand to undertake schemes in what he called his 'Houses of Parliament' style.

In order to carry out the work effectively and to produce the money he needed to build his church at Ramsgate, Pugin turned his association with J G Crace into a business, which could utilise to the full his design patterns on file at Crace, Hardman and Minton. Crace supervised the installation and maintained the standard of workmanship as the quality of the examples at the recent Pugin exhibition demonstrated. Pugin's design incorporated Francis Bernasconi's plaster Gothic vault of 1813 into the overall plan, by covering it with a brilliant polychromatic scheme of heraldic decoration which celebrated the descent of Earl Somers. The Drawing Room demonstrates not only Pugin's vitality as a designer, but also the quality of craftsmanship that had developed under his aegis. John Hardman of Birmingham provided the metalwork and the stained glass, Herbert Minton the tiles and John Gregory Crace the furniture, painted decoration and carpets. The recently restored Gothic Drawing Room at Eastnor remains as Pugin's most complete interior outside the Houses of Parliament.

Reproduced by kind permission of the author, Patric Morrissey, and the Royal Archaeological Institute

FAMILY LINE OF DESCENT

John Somers, Lord Chancellor to
King William III
(b. 1651 - d. 1716)

Mary Somers — Charles Cocks M.P.
(b. 1653 - d. ...)   (b. ... - d.1727)
Sister and heiress
of the Lord Chancellor.

John Cocks — Mary Cocks (cousin)
(b. ... - d.1775)

Elizabeth Eliot — Charles Cocks — Anne Pole
(b. ... - d.1771)   1st Baron Somers   (b.1752 - d.1833)
(b.1725 - d.1806)

Thomas Cocks   James Cocks

(Founders of Cocks and Biddulph bank of Charing Cross,
now absorbed by Barclays Bank.)

John Somers Cocks — Margaret Nash
1st Earl, 2nd Baron   (b.1766 - d.1831)
(b.1762 - d.1841)   (Daughter of Rev.
(Builder of Eastnor Castle)   Treadway Nash, Antiquarian)

Hon. Philip James Somers Cocks — Frances Herbert
(b.1774 - d.1857)   (b. ... - d.1870)
(Descendant of
William the Conqueror)

Hon. Edward Charles
(b.1786 - killed in action 1812)

John Somers Cocks — Lady Caroline Yorke
(b.1788 - d.1852)   (b. ... - d.1852)
2nd Earl, 3rd Baron   (Daughter of 3rd Earl Hardwicke)

Charles Somers Cocks — Virginia Pattle   - 7 Sisters ('Pattledom') of whom
3rd Earl, 4th Baron   (b.1826 - d.1910)   Adeline - Grandmother of Blanche Clogstoun
(b.1819 - d.1883)   Blanche was a ward of G.F. Watts, the artist,
(Designer of Castle   and married Herbert Haldane Somers Cocks, (see below).
interior and collector)   Julia Margaret Cameron, Victorian photographer.
                      Sara Prinsep, hostess.
                      Mia Jackson's daughter married Leslie Stephen and their
                      daughter, Virginia, married Leonard Woolf.

Isabella Caroline — Lord Henry Somerset
(b.1851 - d.1921)   (b.1849 - d.1932)

Adeline (Duchess of Bedford)

Somers Somerset
(b.1874 - d.1945)

Philip Reginald Cocks
5th Baron Somers
(b.1815 - d.1899)

Arthur Herbert Cocks — Emma Eckford
(b.1819 - d.1881)   (b.1830 - d.1914)

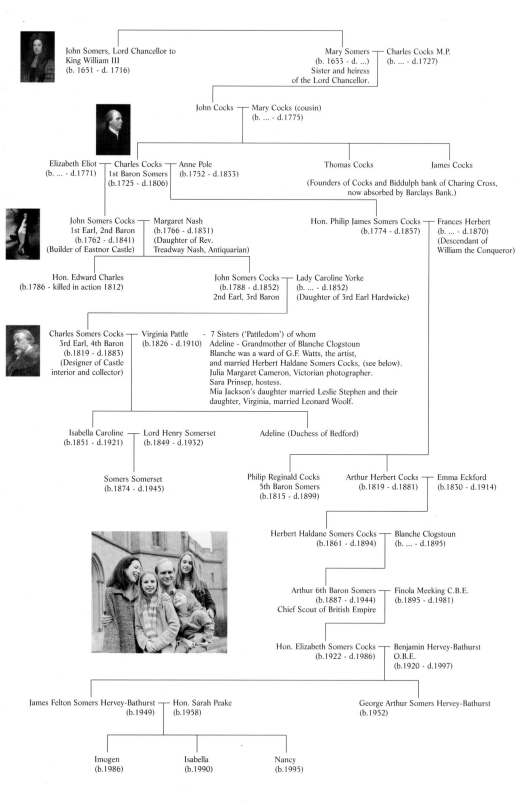

Herbert Haldane Somers Cocks — Blanche Clogstoun
(b.1861 - d.1894)   (b. ... - d.1895)

Arthur 6th Baron Somers — Finola Meeking C.B.E.
(b.1887 - d.1944)   (b.1895 - d.1981)
Chief Scout of British Empire

Hon. Elizabeth Somers Cocks — Benjamin Hervey-Bathurst
(b.1922 - d.1986)   O.B.E.
(b.1920 - d.1997)

James Felton Somers Hervey-Bathurst — Hon. Sarah Peake
(b.1949)   (b.1958)

George Arthur Somers Hervey-Bathurst
(b.1952)

Imogen   Isabella   Nancy
(b.1986)   (b.1990)   (b.1995)